SPORTS BIOGRAPHIES

KEVIN DURANT

KENNY ABDO

Fly!
An Imprint of Abdo Zoom
abdobooks.com

abdobooks.com

Published by Abdo Zoom, a division of ABDO, P.O. Box 398166, Minneapolis, Minnesota 55439. Copyright © 2023 by Abdo Consulting Group, Inc. International copyrights reserved in all countries. No part of this book may be reproduced in any form without written permission from the publisher. Fly!™ is a trademark and logo of Abdo Zoom.

Printed in the United States of America, North Mankato, Minnesota.
102022
012023

Photo Credits: AP Images, Getty Images, iStock, Shutterstock
Production Contributors: Kenny Abdo, Jennie Forsberg, Grace Hansen
Design Contributors: Neil Klinepier

Library of Congress Control Number: 2022937311

Publisher's Cataloging-in-Publication Data

Names: Abdo, Kenny, author.
Title: Kevin Durant / by Kenny Abdo
Description: Minneapolis, Minnesota : Abdo Zoom, 2023 | Series: Sports biographies | Includes online resources and index.
Identifiers: ISBN 9781098280260 (lib. bdg.) | ISBN 9781098280796 (ebook) | ISBN 9781098281090 (Read-to-Me ebook)
Subjects: LCSH: Durant, Kevin, 1988- --Juvenile literature. | National Basketball Association--Juvenile literature. | Brooklyn Nets (Basketball team)--Juvenile literature. | Basketball--Juvenile literature.
Classification: DDC 796.092--dc23

TABLE OF CONTENTS

Kevin Durant 4

Early Years..................... 8

Going Pro...................... 12

Legacy 18

Glossary 22

Online Resources 23

Index 24

KEVIN DURANT

At nearly seven feet (2.1 m) tall, Kevin Durant is a towering power **forward** for the Brooklyn Nets.

Durant has claimed several Most Valuable Player (**MVP**) awards and championship victories as one of the NBA's biggest stars.

EARLY YEARS

Kevin Durant was born in Suitland, Maryland, in 1988. He was a star on the court from the start!

After growing from 6'2" to 6'9" (1.9-2.1 m) in high school, Durant dominated the court. He won the **All-American title** his senior year.

Durant went on to play at the University of Texas. He led the Longhorns to the Big 12 conference his freshman year. After just one year, Durant decided to go pro.

GOING PRO

Durant was immediately selected by the Seattle SuperSonics in the 2007 NBA **draft**. He won the **Rookie** of the Year award that season!

The next year, the SuperSonics became the Oklahoma City Thunder. Durant won three NBA scoring **titles** in a row. He also took the **MVP** title in the 2014 season.

Durant was signed to the Golden State Warriors in 2016. He led the team to win the NBA Finals in 2017. Scoring 39 of the 113 points for his team, Durant **clinched** another **MVP**.

15

In Game 5 of the 2019 NBA Finals, Durant hurt his ankle. He was benched for the rest of the season. During that time, Durant went **free agent**.

Durant signed a four-year contract with the Brooklyn Nets. At the 2021 **Olympics**, he led the U.S. men's basketball team to win the gold against France, scoring 29 points!

LEGACY

18

In 2013, Durant started the Kevin Durant Charity Foundation (KDCF). It supports aid for youth homelessness and disaster relief with education and athletics!

Through trades and injuries, Durant has collected an impressive number of **MVPs** and championships, solidifying his name in NBA history.

GLOSSARY

All-American – awards given annually to the most outstanding athletes in the various sports.

clinch – to confirm a win.

draft – a process in sports to assign athletes to a certain team.

forward – an athlete on a basketball team that plays closest to the opponent's basket.

free agent – a player that does not have a contract with a team and wants to sign with a new team that best suits them.

MVP – short for "most valuable player," an award given in sports to a player who has performed the best in a game or series.

Olympic Games – the biggest international athletic event held as separate winter and summer competitions every four years in a different city.

rookie – a first-year player in a professional sport.

title – a first-place position in a contest.

ONLINE RESOURCES

To learn more about Kevin Durant, please visit **abdobooklinks.com** or scan this QR code. These links are routinely monitored and updated to provide the most current information available.

INDEX

France 17

height 4, 10

injury 16

Kevin Durant Charity Foundation 19

Longhorns (team) 11

Maryland 9

NBA Finals 15, 16

Nets (team) 4, 17

Olympics 17

records 6, 10, 13, 14, 15, 20

SuperSonics (team) 13, 14

Thunder (team) 14

Warriors (team) 15